STATE FLAGS

★ ━━━━━━━━ ★

including the Commonwealth of Puerto Rico

STATE FLAGS

INCLUDING THE COMMONWEALTH OF PUERTO RICO

★ ━━━━━━━━━ ★

BY SUE R. BRANDT

FRANKLIN WATTS

NEW YORK ★ CHICAGO ★ LONDON ★ TORONTO ★ SYDNEY

★ ▬▬▬▬▬ ★

**For Thena and Ryan, Jamie and Jessica
Brett and Chad, Cody and Dylan, Derek
and Patrick, Erin and Teddy**

*The author expresses special thanks
to the secretaries of state and other
officials who generously and most
graciously supplied information on
which the content of this book is based.*

All flags courtesy of Flag Research Center, Winchester, MA.

Library of Congress Cataloging-in-Publication Data

Brandt, Sue R.
State flags / by Sue R. Brandt.
p. cm.—
Includes bibliographical references and index.
Summary: Describes the history, design, and significance of the
fifty state flags.
ISBN 0-531-20001-9
1. Flags—United States—States—History—Juvenile literature.
[1. Flags—United States—States—History.] I. Title.   II. Series.
CR113.2.B73   1992
929.9'2'0973—dc20
92-8948 CIP AC

CONTENTS

★ ■■■■ ★

Also by Sue R. Brandt

FACTS ABOUT THE 50 STATES

HOW TO WRITE A REPORT

STATE TREES
Including the Commonwealth of Puerto Rico

INTRODUCTION

Almost everyone likes to see flags flying in the breeze or carried on poles in parades. Each flag has a special color or colors and a design of some kind that stand for the people who carry it.

The United States and all the other countries of the world have flags. So do all the states of the United States. Armies, cities, companies, schools, clubs—all have flags. Each one of us could have a flag, too, if we wished. People have had flags since ancient times. The very first flags were not made of cloth. They were carved pieces of metal, wood, or leather carried on poles. Flags of this kind were used in Egypt as long as 6,000 years ago.

When we see the flags of the fifty states and the Commonwealth of Puerto Rico, we notice that many of them have the colors red, white, and blue, or at least one or two of these colors. Red, white, and blue are the colors of the United States—those used on the national flag. But some states have other colors for special reasons. One state flag is green.

The designs or pictures on the state flags are alike in some ways but quite different in other ways. Each one tells an interesting story about the state. Sometimes we can guess what the story is about, but often we need help in understanding the meaning of the design or the picture.

More than thirty of the state flags have on them either the picture that is used on the state seal or the entire seal. The state seal is the signature of the state. When we write letters or papers for our schoolwork, we put our signatures, or names, on them. The people of each state elect a governor and other officers to do the work of the state for them. This work includes the writing of many important papers. Officers of the state sign these papers. But state law requires that the seal be used, too, because it stands for the signatures of all the people.

The seals of most of the fifty states are older than the state flags. The states that were once colonies of England had colonial seals. Those that were territories of the United States before they became states had territorial seals.

Seals have been used since ancient times to stand for written signatures. The idea of having one special flag known as the state flag first became popular during the Civil War, in the 1860s. Many different kinds of military flags had been used in the states from earliest times. These were carried by armed forces that defended the state and served in the national army in time of war.

When we learn about the state flags, we also learn about state mottoes. A motto is a saying that helps tell what people believe in. Usually the state motto is a part of the picture on the seal, and often it is written in Latin.

The stories of many of the state flags are long stories, going back to the beginning of the states and sometimes beyond that. It would take many pages to tell all that is known about each flag and the design or picture on it. This book can tell only a bit about each one.

ALABAMA

★ ■■■■■■■■ ★

the Twenty-second State, 1819

Alabama's white flag has a crimson cross shaped like an X on it. The cross reminds the people of Alabama of a well-loved flag that their soldiers and soldiers from other states carried during the Civil War. That flag became known as the Battle Flag of the Confederacy. In the Civil War, Alabama and other Southern states fought against all the other states from 1861 to 1865. The Southern states called themselves the Confederate States of America, or the Confederacy. The causes of the war were slavery and other problems.

After the war, Alabama and some of the other Southern states wanted to have state flags that reminded them of Confederate flags. The Battle Flag had a blue X-shaped cross, with thirteen white stars, on a red background. An X-shaped cross on a flag is called a saltire. A cross of this shape is also sometimes called the cross of St. Andrew. The Battle Flag is on the flags of Georgia and Mississippi.

■■■■■■

State Motto: "We Dare Defend Our Rights"
Flag Adopted: 1895

ALASKA

★ ━━━━━ ★

the Forty-ninth State, 1959

Alaska's flag was designed by a thirteen-year-old schoolboy, Benny Benson. He was in the seventh grade when he entered a contest open to all young people in grades seven through twelve. They were asked to make designs for a flag of Alaska. At that time, Alaska belonged to the United States, but it had not become a state. It was called the territory of Alaska. As the winner of the contest, Benny received a gold watch and a $1,000 scholarship.

Benny explained his design in this way: "The blue field is for the Alaska sky and the forget-me-not, a flower that grows in Alaska. The North Star is for the future state of Alaska, the most northerly in the Union. The Dipper is for the Great Bear—symbolizing strength." The seven stars that make up the constellation of the Big Dipper are in the larger constellation Ursa Major, or the Big Bear. The two stars forming the front of the dipper point toward the North Star, the eighth star on the flag. Benny's flag became the state flag when Alaska became a state. The forget-me-not is the state flower.

━━━━━

State Motto: "North to the Future"
Flag Adopted: 1927

ARIZONA

★ ▬▬▬▬▬▬ ★

the Forty-eighth State, 1912

The big copper-colored star on Arizona's flag stands for copper. Arizona mines more copper than any other state. The star rises against the rays of a setting sun. The thirteen red and yellow rays stand for the first thirteen states. The colors red and yellow are used because these have been the colors of Spain for a very long time. Spain and then Mexico ruled the land that includes Arizona for about 300 years before it became a part of the United States. The people of Arizona are proud of this part of their history. Blue was chosen for the lower half of the flag because blue and gold (yellow) are the state colors of Arizona.

▬▬▬▬

State Motto: "God Enriches"
Flag Adopted: 1917

ARKANSAS

★ ▬▬▬▬▬ ★

the Twenty-fifth State, 1836

Arkansas has a diamond in the center of its flag because Arkansas is the only place in North America where diamonds have been discovered and mined. The twenty-five white stars in the blue band around the diamond mean that Arkansas was the twenty-fifth state to join the Union. One of the four blue stars on the diamond (the one at the top) shows that Arkansas was a member of the Confederate States of America during the Civil War. The other three stars have these meanings: Three countries—Spain, France, and the United States—have ruled the land that includes Arkansas. The United States bought the land from France in 1803 (this land was called the Louisiana Purchase). Arkansas was the third state to be formed from that purchase. The flag was designed by Willie Hocker of Wabbaseka, Arkansas.

▬▬▬▬▬

State Motto: "The People Rule"
Flag Adopted: 1913

The star commemorating the Confederacy was added in 1923, and the four stars in the diamond were arranged in the present form in 1924.

CALIFORNIA

★ ━━━━━━━ ★

the Thirty-first State, 1850

California's flag is called the Bear Flag. It was made by a small group of settlers from the United States who had gone to California while Mexico still governed the land. These settlers wanted to be free from Mexico. In 1846 they marched on the town of Sonoma and made a prisoner of the Mexican officer there. A member of the group, William B. Ide, then issued a statement saying that California was an independent republic. The settlers put a grizzly bear on their flag because the grizzly stands for courage. The idea of a single star may have come from the star called the Lone Star on the flag of the Republic of Texas. But California was never an independent country, as Texas once was. The United States won California and other land in a war with Mexico that ended in 1848, and California became a state soon after that.

State Motto: *"Eureka"* ("I have found it")
Flag Adopted: 1911

The law was rewritten in 1953 to describe all the details of the flag clearly.

COLORADO

★ ━━━━━━━ ★

the Thirty-eighth State, 1876

Colorado has a colorful flag. The big red C stands for Colorado, which means red in Spanish, and for Colorado's well-known nickname, the Centennial State. Colorado has this nickname because it became a state on the centennial (100th anniversary) of the Declaration of Independence. The yellow disk inside the C is for gold, which was discovered in Colorado in 1858, and for sunshine. The blue is for the color of the skies and one of the colors of the Rocky Mountain columbine, the state flower. White stands for snow on the Rocky Mountains and the other color of the state flower. The flag was designed by Andrew C. Carson, author of the book *Colorado, Top of the World*.

━━━━━━━

State Motto: "Nothing Without Providence"
Flag Adopted: 1911

The flag law was amended in 1924 to define the shade of blue
to be used on the flag, and in 1964 to redefine the size of the C.

COMMONWEALTH
OF PUERTO RICO

★ ■■■■■■■■■■■■■■■■ ★

Puerto Rico's red, white, and blue flag was first used in 1895, when Puerto Rico and Cuba rose up against Spain. The white star stood for Puerto Rico. The flag itself represented the spirit of Puerto Ricans who wanted freedom from Spain and the right to take their place in the Americas. After the Spanish-American War in 1898, Spain turned the islands over to the United States.

In 1952, Puerto Rico adopted a form of government with three branches, much like the governments of the fifty states. (The branches are the legislative, the executive, and the judicial.) At that time, the flag took on new meanings. The points of the blue triangle stand for the branches of government. The red stripes represent the blood that nourishes the branches and keeps them strong. The white stripes are for human rights and the freedom of the individual.

"Commonwealth" means that Puerto Rico is a special part of the United States, but not a state of the Union. Puerto Rico calls itself *"Estado Libre Asociado de Puerto Rico"* ("Free Associated State of Puerto Rico").

■■■■■■■■■■■■

State Motto: "John Is His Name"
Flag Adopted: 1952

The motto refers to Puerto Rico's patron saint, John the Baptist.
Columbus named the island *San Juan Bautista* (Saint John the
Baptist) in 1493.

15

CONNECTICUT

★ ━━━━━━━━ ★

the Fifth State, 1788

Connecticut's flag has a field (ground, or background) of azure blue—the blue of an unclouded sky. On this field is a beautiful white shield with three vines, each bearing three bunches of purple grapes. The state motto is on a white ribbon below the shield. This design comes from the state seal, and it tells about the founding of Connecticut as a colony of England. The vines stand for the first settlements, which were made by English people who began to move to what is now Connecticut from Massachusetts in the 1630s. These settlements were thought of as grapevines that had been transplanted (moved from one place to another). The motto means "He Who Transplanted Sustains [Us]." It expresses the colonists' belief that God had transplanted them and would sustain them (take care of them) in their new home.

━━━━━━━━

State Motto: "He Who Transplanted Sustains [Us]"
Flag Adopted: 1897

16

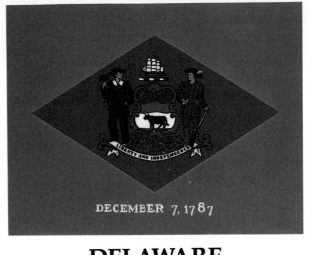

DECEMBER 7, 1787

DELAWARE

★ ■■■■■■■■ ★

the First State, 1787

The date on Delaware's flag, December 7, 1787, is one of the most important in Delaware's long history. On that date, Delaware ratified (approved) the Constitution of the United States. Because it was the first of the original thirteen states to do so, it gained the nickname the First State. The diamond on the flag stands for an earlier nickname, the Diamond State. Delaware was called a "jewel" in colonial and Revolutionary War times. It was small, but like a diamond (or jewel), it was of great worth, especially because of its leaders and its location on the Atlantic Ocean. Buff and blue were chosen as the main colors of the flag because General George Washington and some regiments wore blue coats with buff facings during the Revolutionary War. The picture on the diamond comes from the state seal. It tells about the kinds of work that were important in early times. Some people were farmers (like the figure on the left), some were soldiers, and some worked in the shipping industry.

State Motto: "Liberty and Independence"
Flag Adopted: 1913

FLORIDA

★ ━━━━━━ ★

the Twenty-seventh State, 1845

Florida is a land of sunshine, flowers, palm trees, and rivers and lakes. The picture on the state seal, in the center of the flag, is a scene from early times that shows all these features. There is a brilliant sun, a large palm tree, a steamboat sailing on sparkling waters, and a Native American woman scattering flowers. The picture is basically the same as it was in 1868, when the seal was first adopted, but certain parts have been changed since that time. For instance, the original cocoa tree has been changed to the cabbage palmetto, which became the state tree in 1953. The dress of the woman has been changed to show without question that she represents the Seminoles, Native Americans who have long lived in Florida.

Except for the state seal, Florida's flag may remind us of the flag of Alabama. Both Florida and Alabama were members of the Confederacy during the Civil War.

━━━━━━

State Motto: "In God We Trust"
Flag Adopted: 1899

The flag law was amended in 1900, when the red bars were
added; the seal was last revised in 1985.

GEORGIA

★ ■■■■■■ ★

the Fourth State, 1788

Georgia's flag has two parts. One part is a vertical blue band with the state seal in the center. The other is the Battle Flag of the Confederacy. (The story of Alabama's flag tells about the Battle Flag.) The date in the border of the state seal, 1776, is the date of the Declaration of Independence. The three pillars, or columns, on the seal stand for the three branches, or parts, of government. One branch is the legislature, which makes the laws. Another branch, the executive, headed by the governor or the president, carries out the laws. The third branch (the courts) judges questions about the laws. The arch above the pillars stands for the constitution, on which the laws are based. The words on the ribbons—"wisdom," "justice," and "moderation"—express the principles, or ideals, of the constitution. The design on the seal is like a civics lesson in picture form. The flag was designed by John Sammons Bell, an Atlanta lawyer.

■■■■■■

State Motto: "Wisdom, Justice, Moderation"
Flag Adopted: 1956

HAWAII

★ ▬▬▬ ★

the Fiftieth State, 1959

Hawaii was once an independent kingdom (from 1810 to 1893). The flag that is now the state flag was designed at the request of the first king, Kamehameha I. It has eight stripes of white, red, and blue, along with the flag of Great Britain in the upper left corner. The stripes stand for the eight main islands. The British flag honors Hawaii's friendship with Great Britain. The friendship began when the British explorer Captain James Cook visited the islands in 1778 and named them the Sandwich Islands. In 1794 a British navigator, George Vancouver, presented a British flag to Kamehameha, who was then a warrior chief, and Kamehameha flew it for twenty-two years. During those years, he founded the kingdom and decided that it should have a flag of its own. The new flag was first used in 1816. Early flags usually had nine stripes, which were later reduced to eight.

▬▬▬

**State Motto: "The Life of the Land Is
Perpetuated in Righteousness"
Flag Adopted: 1845**

IDAHO

★ ▬▬▬▬ ★

the Forty-third State, 1890

Idaho's blue flag has the state seal in the center and "State of Idaho" on a red band below the seal. In the picture on the seal, a woman stands on one side of a shield, and a man on the other side. The woman represents liberty, justice, and equality. Beside her are stalks of wheat and syringa, or mock orange, the state flower. The man is a miner. On the shield are mountains, the Snake River, and a pine tree, as well as a farmer plowing a field and buildings near a mine. These pictures suggest that the main industries are forestry, farming, and mining. Below the shield, fruits and vegetables spill out of two cornucopias. A cornucopia, or horn of plenty, stands for abundance. The elk's head represents wildlife. The state motto appears on a ribbon above the elk's head.

▬▬▬▬

State Motto: "Let It Be Perpetual," or "May It Endure Forever"
Flag Adopted: 1907

Until 1927 only the picture from the seal appeared on the flag; details on the seal were revised in 1957.

ILLINOIS

★ ▬▬▬▬▬ ★

the Twenty-first State, 1818

The first thing we notice on the white flag of Illinois is a bald eagle with a streamer in its beak. The eagle stands for the United States. The words on the streamer are the state motto, which means that Illinois governs itself under the government of the United States. We notice, too, that the eagle perches on a boulder and grasps a shield with thirteen bars and thirteen stars. The bars and stars stand for the first thirteen states. The two dates on the boulder are the dates of statehood and of the state seal. The ground around the boulder stands for the state's rich prairie soil. The flag was designed by Lucy Derwent of Rockford, Illinois. She used the picture on the state seal.

▬▬▬▬

State Motto: "State Sovereignty, National Union"
Flag Adopted: 1915

The flag law was amended in 1970 to add the name of the state
and to correct details on the seal.

INDIANA

★ ━━━━━━ ★

the Nineteenth State, 1816

A golden torch burns brightly in the center of Indiana's blue flag. The flames of the torch stand for two things that the people of Indiana believe in most: liberty and enlightenment. The rays that extend out from the torch mean that freedom and knowledge are not just for certain people. They reach out and help make life better for all people. The large gold star above the flame stands for Indiana. The eighteen smaller stars stand for the number of states in the Union before Indiana joined. They are arranged in two groups—thirteen in the outer circle, for the first thirteen states, and five more in the inner circle. The flag was designed by Paul Hadley, of Mooresville, Indiana. He won a contest that was held to obtain a design for the state flag. The contest was part of Indiana's celebration of its 100th birthday in 1916.

State Motto (Slogan): "The Crossroads of America"
Flag Adopted: 1917

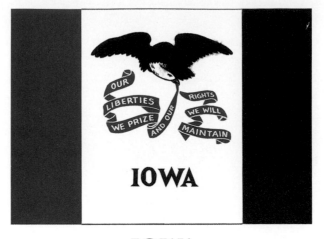

IOWA

★ ━━━ ★

the Twenty-ninth State, 1846

Iowa's flag resembles the flag of France. Both have three vertical stripes of blue, white, and red, arranged in the same order. The French flag flew over what is now Iowa when it was part of a large territory that belonged to France. That territory was called the Louisiana Purchase after the United States bought it from France in 1803. On the white stripe, a beautiful bald eagle flies through the air carrying blue streamers in its beak. The state motto appears on the streamers in white letters. The eagle and the streamers are part of the picture on the state seal. The name of the state, in red letters, is below the eagle. The flag was designed by Mrs. Dixie Cornell Gebhardt of Knoxville, Iowa.

━━━

**State Motto: "Our Liberties We Prize,
and Our Rights We Will Maintain"
Flag Adopted: 1921**

KANSAS

the Thirty-fourth State, 1861

It is not surprising to see a sunflower on Kansas's dark blue flag. The sunflower is the state flower, and Kansas is nicknamed the Sunflower State. The picture below the sunflower comes from the state seal. It shows what was happening in Kansas during the time of the pioneers. A farmer is plowing a field near his log cabin. Covered wagons are moving westward. Native Americans are hunting bison. A steamboat sails on the Kansas River. The thirty-four stars show that Kansas was the thirty-fourth state. The state motto above the stars means that the people of Kansas do not let difficulties keep them from doing their best. The name of the state is in large gold letters below the picture. The American buffalo (bison) is now the state animal, and "Home on the Range" is the state song.

State Motto: "To the Stars Through Difficulties"
Flag Adopted: 1927
The state name was added to the flag in 1963.

KENTUCKY

★ ━━━━━━━━ ★

the Fifteenth State, 1792

Kentucky has placed its seal in the center of its navy blue flag. The two friends in the picture represent all the people, and they are acting out the meaning of Kentucky's motto: "United We Stand; Divided We Fall." They are shaking hands, showing that they work together as friends for the good of all. Sprays of goldenrod, Kentucky's flower, extend around the lower half of the picture. The words "Commonwealth of Kentucky" are on the seal because Kentucky calls itself a commonwealth instead of a state. Massachusetts, Pennsylvania, and Virginia also are known officially as commonwealths. When "commonwealth" is used in this way, it means the same as "state." The word has a different meaning than in the name Commonwealth of Puerto Rico. See *Puerto Rico*.

State Motto: "United We Stand; Divided We Fall"
Flag Adopted: 1918

The flag law was amended in 1928 and 1962 because of changes
in details on the seal.

LOUISIANA

★ ━━━━━━━━ ★

the Eighteenth State, 1812

The pelican has been a symbol of Louisiana since it first appeared on the seal in the early 1800s, when Louisiana was a territory of the United States. The brown pelican is now the state bird, and Louisiana is known as the Pelican State. The pelican has a long bill and a pouch hanging down from the throat and lower jaw. It is a fascinating bird. Long ago, people told strange and wonderful stories about it. In the stories, the pelican often stood for caring and for generosity in helping those in need. Pictures showing the pelican "in the act of tearing its breast to feed its young" became well known, and that is the way it is shown on Louisiana's blue flag. It was said that when food was scarce, the mother bird would stab her breast with her beak and use her blood to feed her young. The state motto appears below the picture.

State Motto: "Union, Justice, and Confidence"
Flag Adopted: 1912

MAINE

★ ━━━━━━ ★

the Twenty-third State, 1820

The picture on Maine's blue flag is called the state coat of arms. It is used on the seal. On the shield in the center, a moose rests under a tall pine tree. The farmer on one side of the shield and the seaman on the other represent the kinds of work the people did in early times. The star is the North Star. People have long used it to tell which direction is north because it points due north to anyone looking at it in the Northern Hemisphere. It directs, or guides, as the state motto, *"Dirigo"* (meaning "I Direct"), says. When the picture was made, Maine was the state farthest north. Maine is nick-named the Pine Tree State. The eastern white pine is the state tree, and the state flower is the cone and tassel of that tree. The moose is the state animal.

━━━━━━━

State Motto: "I Direct," or "I Guide"
Flag Adopted: 1909

MARYLAND

★ ▬▬▬▬▬▬▬▬ ★

the Seventh State, 1788

The people of Maryland are proud of their flag because it reminds them of how Maryland began a long time ago. It was founded as a colony of England in 1634 by Cecil Calvert, who was known as the second Lord Baltimore. His father was the first Lord Baltimore. The designs and the colors on the flag come from Maryland's seal, which was sent from England soon after the first settlement was made. The black and gold (yellow) colors and design stand for the Calvert family. The red and white colors and design stand for the Crossland family. Crossland was the family name of the first Lord Baltimore's mother. Black and yellow are the state colors of Maryland today. We see these colors in the black-eyed Susan, the state flower, and almost the same colors (black and orange) in the feathers of the northern, or Baltimore, oriole, the state bird.

▬▬▬▬▬

State Motto: "Manly Deeds, Womanly Words"
(Motto of the Calvert family)
Flag Adopted: 1904

MASSACHUSETTS

★ ▬▬▬▬▬▬▬▬▬▬▬▬ ★

the Sixth State, 1788

Massachusetts gets its name from a tribe of Native Americans, the Massachuset, who lived around the Blue Hills, south of what is now Boston. The picture on Massachusetts's white flag shows a Native American on a blue shield. He holds a bow in one hand and an arrow in the other. The arrow is pointing downward, standing for friendliness, or peace. The white star represents Massachusetts as one of the first thirteen states. The motto on the blue ribbon around the shield means "By the Sword We Seek Peace, but Peace Only Under Liberty." The arm above the shield holds a sword. It stands for the first part of the motto. The picture, or design, on the flag comes from the seal.

The flag that Massachusetts adopted in 1915 had two designs, one on the front and one on the back. In 1971, the flag law was changed, and the official flag now has only one design, on the front. It is the same as the design on the front of the 1915 flag.

▬▬▬▬▬▬▬▬

**State Motto: "By the Sword We Seek Peace,
but Peace Only Under Liberty"
Flag Adopted: 1971**

MICHIGAN

★ ▬▬▬▬▬▬ ★

the Twenty-sixth State, 1837

The picture on Michigan's blue flag has three mottoes. The one on the white ribbon below the shield is the state motto. It means "If You Seek a Pleasant Peninsula, Look Around." Michigan is made up of two peninsulas. (A peninsula is a landform partly surrounded by water.) In the picture on the shield, a man stands on a peninsula. One of his hands is raised, showing that he wants peace. The other hand rests on a gun to show that peace-loving people are ready to defend their rights. The motto *"Tuebor"* (meaning "I Will Defend") expresses these ideas in words. The elk and the moose stand for Michigan, and the eagle and the motto above the shield represent the United States. The motto—*"E Pluribus Unum,"* meaning "One [Nation] Made Up of Many [States]"—is on the great seal of the United States. The picture was designed for the state seal by Lewis Cass, who was a governor of Michigan territory and later a nationally known political leader.

▬▬▬▬▬▬▬

**State Motto: "If You Seek a Pleasant Peninsula,
Look Around"
Flag Adopted: 1911**

MINNESOTA

★ ▬▬▬▬▬▬ ★

the Thirty-second State, 1858

One small part of Minnesota, called the Northwest Angle, is the place that is farthest north in the first forty-eight states. The words on the flag, *"L'Etoile du Nord,"* are French for "The Star of the North," or "The North Star." That is the state motto and one of Minnesota's nicknames. The motto is on the state seal, along with the picture below it, which shows Minnesota in early times. A pioneer farmer is plowing, and a Native American is hunting. The stump with an ax in it and the pine trees stand for lumbering. The trees also stand for the state tree, the red pine. The blue band around the picture has a wreath of pink and white lady's slippers on it (the state flower) and a ribbon with dates that are important in Minnesota's history. On the white outer band, there are groups of stars, nineteen in all. They show that Minnesota was the nineteenth state to be added to the Union after the original thirteen.

▬▬▬▬▬▬▬

State Motto: "The Star of the North"
Flag Adopted: 1957

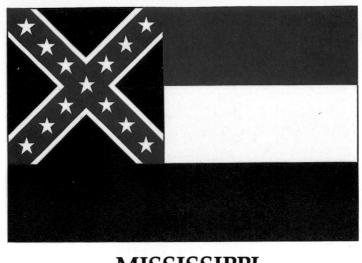

MISSISSIPPI

★ ▬▬▬▬▬▬▬ ★

the Twentieth State, 1817

Mississippi's flag reminds us of the flag of Georgia. Both have the Battle Flag of the Confederacy on them. It also reminds us of the flags of Alabama and Florida, which have an X-shaped cross like the cross on the Battle Flag. The story of Alabama's flag in this book tells about the Battle Flag. It is in the upper left corner of Mississippi's flag. The thirteen stars on it stand for the first thirteen states. The colors blue, white, and red are used in the rest of the flag because these are the colors of the United States flag.

▬▬▬▬▬▬

State Motto: "By Valor and Arms"
Flag Adopted: 1894

MISSOURI

★ ■■■■■■■■■ ★

the Twenty-fourth State, 1821

The picture that is on Missouri's seal appears in the center of the red, white, and blue flag. It is encircled by a blue band with twenty-four white stars, standing for the number of states in 1821. The stars at the top of the picture have the same meaning. The circular shield in the center has two parts. The national part, on the right, comes from the great seal of the United States. The state part has a moon, representing Missouri as a new state, and a grizzly bear. The bear stands for courage, as do the two huge grizzlies that support the shield. Around the shield there is a big white belt with the motto "United We Stand; Divided We Fall." (This motto is also on Kentucky's flag.) The belt and the motto bind the state and the nation together. The state motto is below the shield, along with the date 1820 in Roman numerals. This is the date of the first state constitution. The flag was designed by Mrs. Marie Elizabeth Oliver, of Cape Girardeau, Missouri.

■■■■■■■■

**State Motto: "Let the Welfare of the People
Be the Supreme Law"
Flag Adopted: 1913**

MONTANA

★ ▬▬▬▬▬▬ ★

the Forty-first State, 1889

The name of the state in large gold letters makes Montana's blue flag easy to recognize. The picture below the name comes from the state seal. It shows some of Montana's beautiful scenery and tells what people were doing in pioneer times. The miner's pick and shovel and the plow stand for mining and farming. In the background, a brilliant sun rises over mountains, forests, and the Great Falls of the Missouri River near what is now the city of Great Falls. The state motto, in Spanish, at the bottom of the picture means "Gold and Silver." It was inspired by the discovery of gold in Montana in the early 1860s. Before it was adopted as the state flag, the present flag had been a military flag. It was carried by the First Montana Infantry in the Spanish-American War in 1898.

State Motto: "Gold and Silver"
Flag Adopted: 1905
The name of the state was added in 1981.

NEBRASKA

★ ▬▬▬▬▬▬ ★

the Thirty-seventh State, 1867

Nebraska's flag has a field of national blue with the state seal in gold and silver in the center. The picture on the seal shows that Nebraska was a busy place in the early years of statehood. The man in the foreground is a blacksmith. He is using a hammer and anvil to make horseshoes and other articles from metal. The settler's cabin and the sheaves of wheat stand for farming. A steamboat is sailing up the Missouri River, and the train is following the route of the first transcontinental railroad, which was built westward from Omaha, beginning in 1865. This was the route through the Platte River valley that had been used by pioneer wagon trains and the Pony Express. The train is heading for the Rocky Mountains, which are shown at the far left, although the Rockies are not in Nebraska.

▬▬▬▬▬

State Motto: "Equality Before the Law"
Flag Adopted: 1925

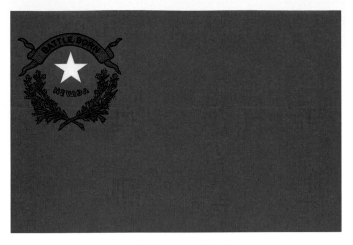

NEVADA

★ ▬▬▬▬▬ ★

the Thirty-sixth State, 1864

Nevada calls itself the Battle Born State because it became a state during the Civil War. It is also known as the Sagebrush State and the Silver State. The large silver star in the upper left corner of the cobalt blue flag stands for silver, the state metal. Sagebrush, the state flower, also appears on the flag in a half wreath around the star. The letters of the name Nevada are arranged around the points of the star, and the words "Battle Born" are on a golden ribbon at the top of the design. Mining of silver and gold was Nevada's main industry in early times. The famous Comstock Lode, which was discovered near Virginia City in 1859, was one of the richest deposits of these metals ever found. Nevada still ranks high among the states in the production of copper, gold, and other metals. Silver and gold are the state colors.

▬▬▬▬

State Motto: "All for Our Country"
Flag Adopted: 1929

NEW HAMPSHIRE

★ ▬▬▬▬▬▬▬▬▬▬ ★

the Ninth State, 1788

The picture on the state seal in the center of New Hampshire's blue flag goes back to Revolutionary War times. It shows the *Raleigh*, which was built at Portsmouth in 1776, as one of the warships of what was to be the United States Navy. The flag on the ship is the nation's flag as it looked in 1777. The water stands for the harbor of Portsmouth, and the rising sun shows that Portsmouth was an important shipbuilding center during the Revolutionary War. In the lower left part of the picture, there is a small granite boulder. New Hampshire is nicknamed the Granite State. Granite, a strong and long-lasting kind of rock, stands for New Hampshire's rugged landscape and the sturdy character of its people. The picture on the seal is surrounded by a wreath of laurel leaves, and the seal on the flag has another wreath of laurel around it, with nine stars standing for the first nine states. The date on the seal, 1776, is the date of the Declaration of Independence.

▬▬▬▬▬▬▬

State Motto: "Live Free or Die"
Flag Adopted: 1909
Details on the seal were revised in 1932.

NEW JERSEY

★ ▬▬▬▬▬▬▬▬ ★

the Third State, 1787

New Jersey is proud of the buff color of its flag. The coats of the uniforms that General George Washington and New Jersey troops wore during the Revolutionary War had buff facings. The picture on the flag comes from the state seal. The women are goddesses from long ago. They stand for the words of the state motto, "Liberty and Prosperity." The goddess Liberty holds a pole with a Liberty Cap, which also stands for liberty, or freedom. The Roman goddess of agriculture, Ceres, stands for agriculture, or farming, which helped bring prosperity to New Jersey in early times. She holds a cornucopia, or horn of plenty. The three plows also stand for agriculture. The helmet shows that New Jersey governs itself. The horse's head stands for the horse as an animal that has long been important for its strength and speed in peace and war. The horse is now the state animal. The date on the flag, 1776, is the date of the Declaration of Independence. Buff and Jersey blue are New Jersey's state colors.

▬▬▬▬▬▬

State Motto: "Liberty and Prosperity"
Flag Adopted: 1896

Details on the seal were revised in 1928.

NEW MEXICO

★ ▬▬▬▬▬▬▬ ★

the Forty-seventh State, 1912

On the yellow field of New Mexico's flag we see a red sun with red rays stretching out from it. There are four groups of rays, with four rays in each group. This is the ancient sun symbol of a Native American people called the Zia, who live in the Zia Pueblo (village) in New Mexico. The design shows what the Zia of long ago believed. They thought that the Giver of All Good Gifts gave them in groups of four. These gifts are the four directions (north, east, south, and west), the year (with its four seasons), the day (with sunrise, noon, evening, and night), and life itself (with childhood, youth, the middle years, and old age). All these are bound together in a circle of life and love, which is without beginning or end. The red and yellow colors are the colors of Spain. Spanish explorers first brought the colors to what is now New Mexico in 1540. The design was suggested by Dr. Harry Mera, a Santa Fe physician and archaeologist. Mrs. Mera made the flag.

▬▬▬▬▬

State Motto: "It Grows As It Goes"
Flag Adopted: 1925

NEW YORK

★ ──────── ★

the Eleventh State, 1788

Parts of the picture on New York's blue flag remind us of the Statue of Liberty, in New York Harbor. The goddess Liberty (on the left side of the shield) holds a pole with a Liberty Cap, which stands for liberty, or freedom. At her feet is a discarded crown, representing freedom from England at the end of the Revolutionary War. The other goddess, Justice, wears a blindfold and holds the scales of justice in one hand. The blindfold and the scales mean that everyone receives equal treatment under the law. The state motto on the white ribbon expresses the idea of reaching upward for higher goals. On the shield, a sun rises over a mountain believed to be in the Hudson Highlands and ships sail on the Hudson River. Above the shield, an eagle perches on a globe representing the New World, or the Western Hemisphere. The picture, called the state coat of arms, was created for use on the seal.

State Motto: *"Excelsior"* ("Ever Upward," or "Still Higher")
Flag Adopted: 1901

41

NORTH CAROLINA

★ ──────────── ★

the Twelfth State, 1789

North Carolina has on its flag its initials and two dates that are important in its history. Both are the dates of meetings that were held in North Carolina not long before the thirteen colonies declared their independence on July 4, 1776. On the first date, May 20, 1775, a group of people met at Mecklenburg and wrote a paper in which they declared their independence. This paper is called the Mecklenburg Declaration of Independence. On the other date, April 12, 1776, North Carolina's lawmakers met at Halifax and prepared a paper called the Halifax Resolves. It told North Carolina's delegates to the Continental Congress, in Philadelphia, to join with the delegates from all the other colonies in declaring independence. The two dates and the initials, with a white star between them, appear on a vertical band of blue. From this band, two broad bands, one red and one white, extend across the flag.

State Motto: "To Be Rather Than to Seem"
Flag Adopted: 1885

NORTH DAKOTA

★ ━━━━━━━━━━━ ★

the Thirty-ninth State, 1889

The picture on North Dakota's flag is similar to the picture on the great seal of the United States. It shows a bald eagle holding an olive branch and a bundle of arrows in its claws. The olive branch stands for peace, and the arrows stand for the power to make war if war is necessary. In its beak, the eagle carries a ribbon with words meaning "One nation made up of many states." The shield on its breast has thirteen stripes, standing for the first thirteen states. The fan-shaped design above the eagle—with thirteen stars and the rays of a brilliant sun—represents the rising of a new nation, the United States. The name North Dakota appears on a red scroll below the eagle. A flag of the same design as the present state flag was carried by the First North Dakota Infantry in the Spanish-American War.

━━━━━━━━━━━

State Motto: "Liberty and Union Now and Forever, One and Inseparable"
Flag Adopted: 1911

OHIO

★ ▬▬ ★

the Seventeenth State, 1803

Everyone notices the shape of Ohio's flag. A flag with this shape is called a burgee. The large blue triangle on the flag stands for Ohio's hills and valleys, and the red and white stripes for roads and waterways in the state. Thirteen of the white stars in the triangle represent the first thirteen states. The others (in the peak of the triangle) are for the next four states, including Ohio, to join the Union. The large white circle suggests the O in the name Ohio, and the red disk inside the circle is a reminder of Ohio's famous nickname, the Buckeye State. The name comes from the large round seeds of the Ohio buckeye tree (the seeds are brown, not red). Native Americans thought that the seeds looked like the eyes of a white-tailed buck deer, and they called the tree the buckeye. It is the state tree, and the white-tailed deer is the state animal. The flag was designed by John Eisenmann, an architect and engineer.

▬▬▬

State Motto: "With God, All Things Are Possible"
Flag Adopted: 1902

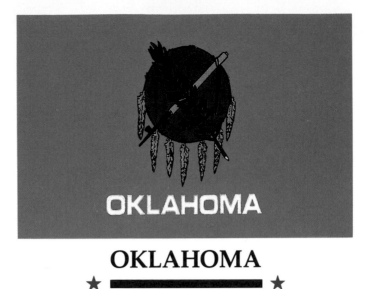

OKLAHOMA

★ ▬▬▬▬▬▬▬▬ ★

the Forty-sixth State, 1907

Before Oklahoma became a state, it was made up of sections called Indian Territory and Oklahoma Territory. Oklahomans of today include more than sixty different groups of Native Americans. The state flag honors them and their ancestors. The blue field comes from a flag carried by Choctaw soldiers during the Civil War. The shield in the center is the battle shield of an Osage warrior of long ago. It is made of buffalo (bison) hide and is decorated with eagle feathers. Two symbols of peace lie across the shield. One is the calumet, or peace pipe, of Native Americans. The other is an olive branch, which has long been used by non–Native Americans to stand for peace. They are placed on top of the shield to show that all the people want peace rather than war. The crosses on the shield are Native American signs for stars, standing for high ideals. The flag was designed by an artist, Mrs. Louise Funk Fluke, of Oklahoma City.

State Motto: "Labor Conquers All Things"
Flag Adopted: 1925

The flag law was amended in 1941 to add the name of the state,
and in 1988 to define the exact color of the field and different
parts of the design.

45

OREGON

★ ▬▬▬▬ ★

the Thirty-third State, 1859

The flag of Oregon, the Beaver State, is the only two-sided state flag now in use. A picture of a beaver, the state animal, appears on the back. The front has the picture used on the state seal, with the words "State of Oregon" above it and the date of statehood below. The field of each side is blue, and the design is in gold. The picture from the seal includes a heart-shaped shield with an eagle on top, surrounded by thirty-three stars, which stand for the number of states in 1859. The scene on the shield shows Oregon when it first became a state. The sun shines over the Pacific Ocean, mountains and forests, and a covered wagon. The plow, wheat, and pickax stand for farming and mining. The two ships represent an important part of Oregon's history. In earlier times, both Great Britain and the United States claimed a large area of land called Oregon Country. In 1846 they divided it between them, and Oregon became a part of the United States. One ship is a British ship leaving Oregon. The other is a United States ship arriving. The eagle stands for the United States, and the motto means that Oregon supports the Union, or the United States. Navy blue and gold are the state colors.

▬▬▬▬

State Motto: "The Union"
Flag Adopted: 1925

PENNSYLVANIA

★ ▬▬▬▬▬▬▬▬ ★

the Second State, 1787

Philadelphia was once the national capital, from 1790 to 1800. Today, Independence National Historical Park in that city is like a huge museum, with exhibits that tell the story of the founding of the United States. The design on Pennsylvania's blue flag goes back to the 1770s. It consists of a shield with an eagle (representing the United States) at the top, and an olive branch and a stalk of corn crossed at the bottom. The shield is supported by rearing black horses, harnessed in red. They stand on golden scrollwork with a red ribbon bearing Pennsylvania's motto. The shield has three sections. The ship in the upper part represents the great amount of trade that Pennsylvania has carried on around the world during its long history. The plow in the middle stands for different kinds of implements, or tools, used in farming and other work. The sheaves of wheat symbolize wealth from abundant harvests, as well as the kind of wealth that comes from human thought and action. The shield appears on the seal, and the whole design is called the coat of arms of the Commonwealth of Pennsylvania.

▬▬▬▬▬▬

State Motto: "Virtue, Liberty, and Independence"
Flag Adopted: 1907

RHODE ISLAND

★ ▬▬▬▬▬▬▬▬▬▬▬ ★

the Thirteenth State, 1790

Rhode Island—often called Little Rhody—is the state with the smallest area and the longest official name: the State of Rhode Island and Providence Plantations. On the white field of the state flag is a circle of thirteen gold stars surrounding a ship's anchor, in gold. The state motto is on a blue ribbon below the anchor. White and blue flags were carried by Rhode Island soldiers beginning in Revolutionary War times. Stars representing the first thirteen states also appeared on early flags. An anchor and the motto "Hope" have been used on the seal from colonial days. No one knows exactly why. An anchor was placed on the colonial seal in 1647, soon after the English government granted a charter to the settlers of Providence Plantations. Perhaps they thought of the charter as an anchor for the new colony. The motto was added after the settlers received a second charter, which gave them the freedom to worship as they pleased. That was what they had hoped for. Possibly the idea of the anchor and the motto came from a biblical (New Testament) quotation, " . . . Which hope we have as an anchor of the soul. . . . " (Hebrews 6:19)

▬▬▬▬▬▬▬▬

State Motto: "Hope"
Flag Adopted: 1897

SOUTH CAROLINA

★ ▬▬▬▬▬▬▬▬▬ ★

the Eighth State, 1788

South Carolina's soldiers needed a flag to carry during the Revolutionary War, and Colonel William Moultrie made one for them. He used the blue color of their uniforms as the field of the flag. He placed on it a silver crescent, or new moon, which the soldiers wore on the front of their caps. At about this time, the people of Charleston heard that British warships planned to capture Sullivan's Island, in the harbor of Charleston, and use it as a base to attack the city. Colonel Moultrie and others quickly built a fort of palmetto logs on the island. When the warships came, the captain and his soldiers defeated them, partly because the cannonballs that the ships fired could not destroy the fort. Instead, they sank into the soft, tough logs. This battle, known as the Battle of Fort Moultrie, was fought on June 28, 1776. A picture of a palmetto tree was added to the flag later. The cabbage palmetto is now the state tree.

State Mottoes: "Prepared in Mind and Resources"
"While I Breathe, I Hope"
Flag Adopted: 1861

SOUTH DAKOTA

★ ▬▬▬▬▬▬▬▬▬▬ ★

the Fortieth State, 1889

South Dakota has placed its nickname, the Sunshine State, around the state seal on its blue flag. The seal provides a picture of the state and of the kinds of work that the people do. The farmer and the field of corn stand for general farming, and the cattle for ranching and dairying. The buildings show that mining and manufacturing are important. Mining began with gold rushes to South Dakota's famous Black Hills in the 1870s. The trees represent lumbering. The Missouri River winds through the picture, and the Black Hills rise in the distance. The river and the steamboat stand for transportation and trade. The gold band around the seal represents the sun's rays.

The flag that South Dakota adopted in 1909 had the state seal on one side and a blazing sun and the nickname on the other. Since 1963, the official flag has had only one design, on the front.

▬▬▬▬▬▬▬

State Motto: "Under God the People Rule"
Flag Adopted: 1963

TENNESSEE

★ ━━━━━━━ ★

the Sixteenth State, 1796

Tennessee is long and narrow in shape. It stretches from North Carolina on the east to the Mississippi River on the west. The three stars on the flag stand for "the three grand divisions" of the state. These are three different kinds of land-forms—the Great Smoky Mountains and other mountains in the east, highlands in the middle, and lowlands along the Mississippi River. The three sections are known as East, Middle, and West Tennessee. Throughout the history of the state, the people in the different sections have lived in different ways, and sometimes they have not worked together. On the flag, they are bound together in a circle that can never be broken. The flag was designed by LeRoy Reeves of the Third Regiment, Tennessee Infantry. He chose crimson for the field of the flag and blue for the background of the stars. "The final blue bar relieves the sameness of the crimson field," he said, "and prevents the flag from showing too much crimson when hanging limp."

State Motto: "Agriculture and Commerce"
Flag Adopted: 1905

TEXAS

★ ━━━ ★

the Twenty-eighth State, 1845

The big white star on the flag of Texas is called the Lone Star of Texas, and Texas is nicknamed the Lone Star State. This star was first used on flags carried by Texans during a war in the 1830s called the Texas Revolution. At that time, Mexico ruled Texas, but many settlers from the United States were living there. The settlers wanted to be free, and they went to war with Mexico. They lost a famous battle called the Battle of the Alamo, but they won the war. Texas declared its independence in 1836 and became the new Republic of Texas. The flag that is now the state flag was adopted by the Congress of the Republic of Texas in 1839. Texas remained an independent country until it became a state of the United States in 1845. The flag is made up of a broad vertical stripe of blue, with the white star on it, and two broad horizontal stripes, one white and one red. The color blue stands for loyalty, white for purity, and red for bravery.

━━━

State Motto: "Friendship"
Flag Adopted: 1839

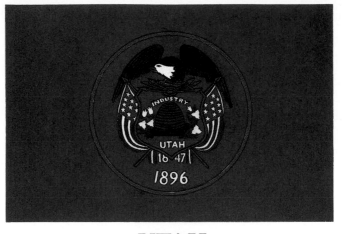

UTAH

★ ▬▬▬ ★

the Forty-fifth State, 1896

Utah is known as the Beehive State, and a beehive is the state emblem. The honeybee is the state insect. The beehive has an important place in the picture on the state seal, which appears on Utah's blue flag. It is in the center of the shield, with a sego lily, the state flower, growing on either side. The sego lily stands for peace. The state motto, "Industry," means industriousness, or steady effort. It refers to the activity of bees in a hive. The national flags in the picture show that Utah supports the United States. The eagle is also a national emblem, standing for protection in peace and war. The date 1847 at the bottom of the shield is very important in Utah's history. In that year, Brigham Young led a group of people to Salt Lake Valley, which was to be their new home. They were members of the Church of Jesus Christ of Latter-day Saints, or Mormons. Soon other Mormons came, and the number of settlements grew. For a while, the Mormons called their land the State of Deseret. Deseret means honeybee.

▬▬▬

State Motto: "Industry"
Flag Adopted: 1913

VERMONT

★ ▬▬▬▬▬▬▬ ★

the Fourteenth State, 1791

The picture on the flag of Vermont, the Green Mountain State, looks like a painting of scenery in that small but beautiful state. It is, in fact, a painting. On the shield in the picture we see a tall pine tree and other trees, a cow, and sheaves of wheat. The Green Mountains are in the distance. Pine boughs extend upward around the shield, and the state motto and the name Vermont are below it. At the top is a stag's head. The painting was made for the state coat of arms. It is based on the state seal, which was designed by Ira Allen and was adopted in 1779. Ira Allen was a brother of Ethan Allen. Both are important in the history of the state. But Ethan Allen is better known because he was the leader of a famous regiment, called the Green Mountain Boys, that fought bravely in the Revolutionary War. Before it became the state flag, the present flag was carried by Vermont soldiers in the Civil War and later wars.

▬▬▬▬▬▬▬

State Motto: "Freedom and Unity"
Flag Adopted: 1923

VIRGINIA

the Tenth State, 1788

Virginia's Latin motto, *"Sic Semper Tyrannis,"* is one of the best known of all the state mottoes. It means "Thus Ever to Tyrants" or, in plain English, "This is what always happens to tyrants [unjust rulers]." It appears on the seal in the center of Virginia's deep blue flag. It was adopted for use on the seal in 1776, when Virginia and the other colonies were fighting for independence from England. The colonies believed that the English government had not treated them justly. To them, England was a tyrant. The two figures in the picture are acting out the meaning of the motto. Both are dressed as warriors of long ago. The woman, Virtue, represents Virginia. The man holds a scourge (whip) and a chain, showing that he is a tyrant. The two have just fought a battle, and the tyrant lies on the ground defeated, with his fallen crown nearby. The motto was suggested by George Mason, who wrote the bill of rights in Virginia's first constitution, adopted in 1776. That bill of rights became the model for the Bill of Rights in the Constitution of the United States.

State Motto: "Thus Ever to Tyrants"
Flag Adopted: 1861

WASHINGTON

★ ━━━━━━━━━━━━━━━━━━ ★

the Forty-second State, 1889

Washington is nicknamed the Evergreen State, and its flag is the only state flag that is green. Washington is named for George Washington, the first president of the United States, and its flag is the only state flag with a picture of a president on it. The state seal on the flag was designed by Charles Talcott, a jeweler in Olympia, Washington. In making the design, Mr. Talcott used an ink bottle and a silver dollar to draw two circles. He had a postage stamp with a picture of George Washington on it, and he pasted the stamp on the inner circle. One of his brothers made the lettering in the outer circle. Another brother prepared the design for use on the seal. Before the present flag was adopted, two other flags had flown over the state. One of these was a military flag with a picture of George Washington in gold on a blue field. The other used the state seal, in gold, on a purple background.

━━━━━━━━━━━━

State Motto: *"Al-Ki"*
Flag Adopted: 1923

(The motto is a Native American expression meaning
"By and By.")

WEST VIRGINIA

★ ▬▬▬▬▬▬▬▬▬▬ ★

the Thirty-fifth State, 1863

West Virginia is called the Mountain State because it has many mountains and hills. Before it became a state, it was the western part of Virginia. The people there wanted to be free—to have their own state. Their wish came true on June 20, 1863. That date is on the rock in the picture on West Virginia's flag. The rest of the design shows what the people were doing and thinking about at that time. The two men stand for farming and mining. Below them on the ground, there are two rifles with a Liberty Cap on top of the rifles. These show that the people were ready to defend their freedom because, as the state motto says, "Mountaineers Are Always Free." Around the picture are a wreath of rhododendron, the state flower, and the name of the state on a red ribbon. The picture was made by an artist, Joseph H. Diss Debar of Doddridge County, for use on the state seal. The white field of the flag is bordered in blue.

▬▬▬▬▬▬

State Motto: "Mountaineers Are Always Free"
Flag Adopted: 1929

WISCONSIN

★ ▬▬▬▬▬▬ ★

the Thirtieth State, 1848

"On, Wisconsin! On, Wisconsin! Grand old badger state! . . . 'Forward,' our motto—God will give thee might!" These words come from Wisconsin's song. The badger is the state animal, and both the badger and the motto appear above the shield on the flag. Wisconsin has water part of the way around it. The sailor and the miner on either side of the shield show that the people work on the water as well as on the land. The shield itself is divided into two main parts. The circular part in the center comes from the great seal of the United States. It means that Wisconsin supports the Union. The state part has four sections with pictures that represent the main industries of Wisconsin—agriculture, mining, manufacturing, and navigation. The cornucopia, or horn of plenty, and the pile of lead stand for farm products and minerals that help bring prosperity. The picture on the flag comes from the seal.

▬▬▬▬▬▬▬▬

State Motto: "Forward"
Flag Adopted: 1913

The flag law was amended in 1979 (effective in 1981) to add the
name of the state and the date of statehood.

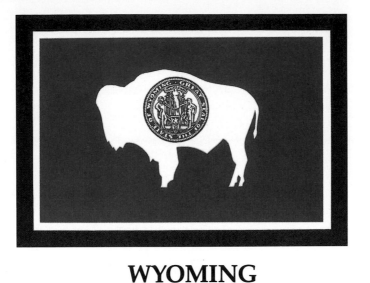

WYOMING

★ ━━━━━━━━━ ★

the Forty-fourth State, 1890

The Cowboy State and the Equality State are two of Wyoming's nicknames. The people of Wyoming know all about cowboys, cattle, and branding cattle. On the flag we see a bison, the state animal, branded with Wyoming's special mark, the state seal. Wyoming is proud of its nickname, the Equality State. It was the first state to give women the right to vote and hold public office. The woman in the picture stands for the state motto, "Equal Rights." The two men represent cattle ranching and mining in early times. The words "Livestock," "Mines," "Grain," and "Oil" tell where Wyoming's wealth comes from today. The eagle and the shield at the bottom show that Wyoming supports the United States. The two dates, 1869 and 1890, tell when Wyoming organized its first government as a territory of the United States and when it became a state. The flag was designed by Mrs. A. C. Keyes of Casper. She placed the bison on a blue field bordered in white and red.

━━━━━━━

State Motto: "Equal Rights"
Flag Adopted: 1917

FOR FURTHER READING

★ ━━━━━━━━━━━━━━━━━━━━ ★

Cannon, Devereaux D., Jr. *The Flags of the Confederacy: An Illustrated History.* Memphis, Tenn.: St. Luke's Press and Bradford Publishing, 1988.

Crampton, William. *The Complete Guide to Flags.* New York: Gallery Books (W. H. Smith Publishers), 1989.

Gebhart, John Robert. *Your State Flags.* Philadelphia: Franklin Publishing, 1973.

Haban, Rita D. *How Proudly They Wave: Flags of the Fifty States.* Minneapolis: Lerner Publications Company, 1989.

Jefferis, David. *Flags.* Easy-Read Fact Book. New York: Franklin Watts, 1985.

Shankle, George E. *State Names, Flags, Seals, Songs, Birds, Flowers, and Other Symbols.* Rev. ed. New York: H. W. Wilson, 1941.

Shearer, Benjamin F., and Shearer, Barbara S. *State Names, Seals, Flags, and Symbols: A Historical Guide.* Westport, Conn.: Greenwood Press, 1987.

Smith, Whitney. *The Flag Book of the United States.* Rev. ed. New York: William Morrow, 1975.

―――. *Flags Through the Ages and Across the World.* New York: McGraw-Hill, 1975.

See encyclopedia articles on flags and seals.

━━━━━━━━━━

INDEX

★ ━━━━ ★